contemporary asian
POOLS AND GARDENS

Karina Zabihi and Chami Jotisalikorn
photos by Luca Invernizzi Tettoni

PERIPLUS

Published by Periplus Editions with
editorial offices at 130 Joo Seng Road
#06-01 Singapore 368357

ISBN 0 7946 0176 6
Printed in Singapore

Distributed by:
North America, Latin America and Europe
Tuttle Publishing, 364 Innovation Drive,
North Clarendon, VT 05759-9436, USA
tel: (802) 773 8930; fax: (802) 773 6993
email: info@tuttlepublishing.com
www.tuttlepublishing.com

Asia Pacific
Berkeley Books Pte Ltd, 130 Joo Seng Road
#06-01/03, Singapore 368357
tel: (65) 6280 1330; fax: (65) 6280 6290
email: inquiries@periplus.com.sg
www.periplus.com

Japan
Tuttle Publishing, Yaekari Building, 3F,
5-4-12 Osaki, Shinagawa-ku,
Tokyo 141-0032
tel: (813) 5437 0171; fax: (813) 5437 0755
email: tuttle-sales@gol.com

the new asian Pools and Gardens:
Bringing Harmony into the Home

Today's tropical garden is constantly pushing the boundaries of contemporary landscape and design while still retaining its essentially Asian heritage and personality. Although inspiration may come from Balinese, Chinese, Japanese or Thai models, the contemporary Asian garden creates its own thoroughly modern idiom by combining traditional elements with bold industrial materials like steel, granito, slate and concrete.

The design of any living space is greatly enhanced by having well thought out landscaping. And whereas the garden was once considered an afterthought to the design of a house, "a place to be viewed rather than to be participated in," according to landscape architect Karl Princic of Bali-based Karl Princic Design, today's modern Asian gardens play a pivotal role in the overall design of the house.

With his Barcelona Pavilion designed for the International Exhibition in Barcelona in 1929, Mies van der Rohe was one of the first architects to incorporate the concept of indoors and outdoors with his open spaces that merged seamlessly with the surrounding landscape.

Perhaps one of the most important developments in recent years is the resurgence of this concept of the garden being another room in the house, which has been explored by a number of architects including John Pawson and Sri Lankan architect Geoffrey Bawa, for whom the garden was "a series of rooms seen in succession or as a whole." His architecture was inseparable from the surrounding environment. His garden at Lunuganga and his house in Colombo are cases in point.

More and more people are taking the time to think as much about the design of their gardens as they are about the design of their homes. This stems in some part from the explosion of spa resorts in Asia. These havens of tranquility offer luxurious escapes where nature is definitely part of the nurturing process.

Renowned Mexican architect Luís Barragan referred to himself as a landscape architect. In *Contemporary Architects* he wrote, "I believe that architects should design gardens to be used, as much as the houses they build, to develop a sense of beauty and the taste and inclination toward the fine arts and other spiritual values. Any work of architecture which does not express serenity is a mistake."

Garden design is progressively emulating architecture and art. In a way we are urbanizing our gardens and more importantly, as the following pages show, gardens are moving into the house and vice versa. As Karl Princic says, "the essence of garden design is the successful blurring of boundaries between outdoors and indoors. It is now difficult to imagine any project without the influence of landscape."

While homeowners ultimately seek beautiful landscapes, they are also demanding gardens that are easy to maintain, hence the introduction of streamlined gardens.

We are seeing fewer flower beds—restraint in the variety of plants often focuses the attention and enhances a space —and more sculpted gardens that adhere to the Japanese principle of *shakkeii*, or "borrowed scenery,"—a concept that draws the surrounding landscape into the garden. The principles of *shakkeii* work well regardless of the size of the garden, and are therefore ideally suited to urban living.

One of the most recurring themes is the existence of water. According to Stan and Geri Lee, the owners of Singapore-based landscape design company Watermount Gardens, "water is a key element in the Asian garden. Incorporating a water feature adds life to the garden whether it is in the form of a pond, a simple or elaborate water feature or rock pool."

The garden and pool of this house in Singapore designed by Italian team Sottsass Associati illustrate a striking contemporary style. The bold lines of the house and blue tiles are mirrored in the enormous pool that dominates the landscape. Plants are kept to a minimum with potted greens and a low hedge.

Swimming pools are the ultimate symbol of a leisurely life. Think hot, hot days with a cool, cool drink, the smell of suntan lotion and the gentle sound of splashing water. A swimming pool undoubtedly enhances the quality of life. Unlike in the colder climates of Europe or North America, swimming pools in Asia are used all year round. Apart from the health benefits of swimming, the pool is a great way to keep children amused and the perfect backdrop for entertaining. And what better way to unwind than jumping in a pool after a hard day's work?

Once upon a time in the not too distant past, swimming pools were exclusively the domain of the rich, due in part to prohibitive costs. Today however, private swimming pools are increasingly a feature of modern living spaces—and you don't necessarily have to live in a house to have one. With more cost effective construction and better technology, pools are increasingly appearing in apartments as plunge pools or as a design feature of a penthouse apartment.

The pool plays an important part in our lives in tropical Asia —for relaxing, cooling, exercising, entertaining or as a reflective artistic feature of the house. Whether it is a large outdoor pool, indoor lap pool or a rooftop eyrie, unusual shapes and designs that reflect the geometry of the house are much in vogue. Examples include Valentina Audrito's pools in a Bali villa (pages 72 and 78) or the pools by Eco-id Architects in Singapore which form an integral part of a living room (pages 42 and 110) or the pools in a villa in Kanchanaburi in Thailand designed by Martin Palleros (pages 123–124) which merge seamlessly with the landscape. The serenity of the Tirtha wedding chapel in Bali (page 80) is much enhanced by its setting in a vast lake.

What makes a tropical garden intrinsically different from gardens anywhere else in the world is that with our climate we can spend more time in them all year round. As Karl Princic

left The positioning of the pool in the central courtyard with the draping, white flowered frangipani tree weaves an intimate and tranquil spell over this Singapore house. The single splash of color is provided by the rich *Cordyline fruticosa* or ti plant.
below Abundant greenery is offset by the clean lines of stone to create a thoroughly modern urban pool area at the Downtown Apartments in Bali.

explains, "historically, tropical Asian houses have always been designed to take advantage of natural breezes and therefore the garden has always been an extension of the house." The advent of air-conditioning meant that for a time the garden was excluded from the house. Happily that is all changing. Al fresco dining is increasingly popular with open-plan kitchens and dining rooms becoming part of the garden or patio—a popular idea in Australia and New Zealand, and is now catching on in the rest of the region. With cantilevered roofs and sophisticated waterproof canopies that can be easily adjusted according to the vagaries of the weather, more people are embracing it.

The design of garden furniture is likewise making great leaps. Rather than the once ubiquitous plastic chairs and tables, retailers like X•TRA Resort and Natural Living in Singapore are stocking aesthetically pleasing dining furniture, loungers, sun parasols and lighting that accentuate and enhance the garden

right Simple arrangements of plants can often make as dramatic a statement as colorful exotics. These tree ferns enhance the sculptured stonework that frames the entrance to the villas at Downtown Apartments in Bali.

below Bangkok's first vertical garden, located in Extase restaurant at H1 Complex, is an indoor garden created entirely of vertical plants designed as foliate wall. Natural sunlight enters through the glass roof, which shelters the diners beneath.

opposite The rectangular shapes of these shallow pools are softened by low shrubs and tropical ferns, enhancing the tranquil atmosphere of this special space, and infusing it with a quiet buzz of organic energy.

Gardens often define a country more readily than does architecture. Pools, fountains, pavilions and pergolas were a natural part of eastern, Roman, Arab, and Greek civilizations. The Taj Mahal with its pools and gardens was considered "paradise on earth." Think of Versailles and the predominant image is one of order, where everything is laid out in straight, parallel lines. Think of an English garden and the image is one of "chaotic order," where the seasons inspire the plants and flowering shrubs. A traditional Chinese garden incorporates the four main elements of water, stone, plants and architectural structures—elements that with their contrasting *yin* and *yang* combine to create harmony. Be it a traditional Chinese or Japanese or Balinese garden, the emphasis is on creating a space that is peaceful and tranquil—a place for quiet contemplation. Echoing this theme of tranquility and a balm for the mind as well as the body, many public gardens in Singapore now incorporate "healing" features such as reflexology paths. The landscaping around Eckard Rempe's health resort at San Benito reflects the alternative therapies available at The Farm.

The inspiration for the garden designs of today come from many different quarters, from historical contexts, to modern architecture, from the play of light and shadow to the ripples of water and, of course, plants and trees. The contemporary

right Think of the tropics and the image of majestic palm trees swaying in the ocean breeze immediately springs to mind. This large garden in Bali provides the ideal setting for these coconut palms. Their height allows for uninterrupted views of the ocean beyond while also gracefully framing the infinity pool. Natural wood decking and a lounger enclosed in muslin drapes add a touch of romance.
below The pool at Villa Surga in Bali designed by Valentina Audrito echoes the architectural footprint of the house.

Asian garden is concerned with bringing harmony into the home yet it is also concerned with imbuing a sense of adventure in the vernacular design.

What is also exciting is that there is no one singular style. Instead, architects and designers are experimenting with form and volume, combining traditional motifs with a contemporary idiom. Examples of this is seen in the Balinese *balés* given a modern make-over, or Chinese statutes set against contemporary structures. Perhaps inspired by the blurring of inside and outside, landscape architects are experimenting with industrial materials such as steel, iron, glass and concrete in the modern Asian gardens. As Geri and Stan say, "Garden design can be taken to a different level by tastefully merging 'funky or quirky' materials with the correct plant types to enhance them."

Gardens in land-scarce Singapore and Bangkok are by necessity smaller, more intimate and enclosed whereas the opposite is true in Bali where rural gardens are more spacious.

left This urban garden in Bangkok recreates the romance of
Bali with a picturesque fountain
made of Balinese wooden rice
pounders. The pond is filled with
an exotic profusion of water lilies,
lotuses, fish and terrapins.
below A square fountain in
solid black stone gives solemn
serenity to the entrance of the
spa at The Farm at San Benito
in the Philippines.

But a garden, no matter how small, is obviously an asset.
Even in a shophouse or on the rooftop or balcony of a
condominium, interesting "gardens" can be created by the
judicious inclusion of water features and plants. The urban
gardens lend themselves to the concept of "secret gardens"
with different levels, hideaways, nooks and crannies, path-
ways and even miniature labyrinths.

A successful garden achieves functionality, sensuality and
architectural balance. Creating an aesthetically pleasing garden
requires a degree of choreography, an obvious knowledge of
what plants work well in certain conditions and an appreciation
of perspective. Plants and foliage of course play an important
role in the garden but it is how these plants interact with the
rest of the house and reflect both the architecture and the
owners' personality that matters. Many of the tropical Asian
plants and trees we think of as native species in fact were
collected by intrepid explorers and transported to Europe (for
exhibition in hothouses like Kew Gardens) or taken to Asia. The
frangipani, a New World native, now proliferates in Thailand

right Architects and designers are creating ever more imaginative concepts for railings and gates such as these eye-catching individual iron posts surrounding The Equatorial in Singapore.
below In this house in Singapore, the contrasting materials like stone and metal railings and the varied levels make for an alluring entrance to the garden.

and Malaysia. The bougainvillea, originally from Brazil, was named after French explorer Louis Antoine de Bougainville, who brought the plant to other warm parts of world in the 18th century.

Today's gardens borrow from the latest innovations in pool design, fencing and gates, paving and meandering paths. Secret nooks, water features and carefully placed lighting all play an integral part in any contemporary landscaping, as do artwork—a new element in Asian gardens. Whether it is a family heirloom, modern sculpture or an elaborate fountain, this artwork provides a focal point and dramatic visual statement in the garden. Karl Princic adds, "Temples, shrines and artifacts are very much part of Asian culture and these are often prominent features of new and old garden designs."

A garden, perhaps more than a house, requires constant maintenance. It does not always remain the same. It changes, becomes run down and overgrown, dies and is reborn. The east is extraordinary fecund, where luscious plants defy our attempts to subdue them. After just one rainy season, gardens become overgrown—nature simply takes over. But having a precious green space is well worth the effort; to quote an old Chinese proverb, "he who plants a garden plants happiness."

thai seed Designed by Bill Bensley of Bensley Design Studios, the lush tropical landscaping of Anantara Resort & Spa Hua Hin is inspired by the classic elements of traditional Thai landscape and architecture, reinterpreted in contemporary style.

left A series of plants is used to break the lawn space into visual and textural planes. A gradual layering of horizontal planes is created from the ground upward, starting with flat grass, low spiky bushes, moving higher with a flat hedge, and culminating in the conical points of small trees.
below A trellised loggia links the hotel entrance to a side driveway. At the far end, the image of a celestial being from Thai mythology adds the classical element.
opposite The hotel rooms are positioned along man-made canals that were landscaped to evoke life along the waterway— an intrinsic element of rural Thai culture. At left a *sala*, or open-air Thai pavilion like those used as boat landings in the countryside, forms the entrance to a wooden bridge. A leaf motif on the pebbled footpath adds contemporary charm to counterbalance the classic architecture.

left This simple wooden walkway outside the spa suites resembles typical rural walkways along the waterways in the Thai countryside. A massive love seat beckons at the ond of the path.
opposite The resort's infinity edge pool merges into the liquid horizon of a vast man-made lagoon covered with water lilies that again harkens to Thailand's native water culture. The dramatic, fortress-like facade of the spa wing on the left adds a majestic backdrop to the scene.

right A gentle gradation of the swimming pool's infinity edge gives it a natural flow into the lagoon, so that the pool merges quietly into the environment.
far right top Oil burners along the wooden walkway provide lighting that is both romantic and dramatic.
far right below Each spa suite door is flanked by water vessels that offer a floral welcome of local blossoms.

natural balance Designed by owner and founder, Eckard Rempe, The Farm at San Benito is a health resort for alternative medicine, featuring private gardens, massage huts and meditation *balés* spread over nine hectares of lushly landscaped grounds.

opposite A wooden deck melds easily with the natural surroundings; at The Farm, the man-made elements and natural landscape merge into an integrated whole.

opposite right The dining experience, set against a lush, leafy backdrop that evokes the site's tropical jungle environment, is in tune with nature.

opposite far right A geometric pattern made from weathered wooden planks set in a concrete base creates an elegantly textured path.

above The entrance courtyard to the spa is a zone of of zen-like tranquility. Gray and black stones create a mood of solemn serenity, anchored by a dramatic black stone fountain in the center. The doorway and fountain are centered to create an experience of balanced calm, enhanced by the perfectly matched frangipani trees that flank the fountain.

right A Japanese-flavored koi scale pattern is among the many Asian motifs that appear in the landscape design.

top and above Shallow stone steps form an easily ascendable approach to the Salus per Aqua Spa and jungle gym.

left The Farm is located in the foothills of Mount Malarayat in Lipa, the Philippines, within view of the mountain range. Dawn's misty light lends a magical glow to the carpet of moss covering this romantic corner designed for casual outdoor dining. The star of the show is a giant, 200-year-old mango tree draped with picturesque hanging moss.

right This funky stone footpath is one of the many creative paths that form a network of walkways connecting the numerous gardens spread over the grounds.

artscape When it came to designing their villa in Bali, Philip Lakeman and Graham Oldroyd wanted the garden to feature as a strong element within that design and for "the outside landscape to feel and function as if it were another room in the house."

above Originally hailing from Mexico, *Russelia equisetiformis* or the firecracker plant gives the impression of an "ordered wilderness" to this section of Philip and Graham's garden. Clusters of bright red flowers accentuate the high terracotta wall while pots filled with yucca plants add yet another tier and draw attention to the Alang Alang roof beyond.

right Fish-like sculpted urns created by the artists line the pathway to the main house. A doorway made of a large rusted metal roller provides a dramatic entrance. The terracotta facade of the walls lends itself to the artists' concept of mixing cultures and traditions to create a "one world"-style house and garden.

above The artists' gardens provide a cornucopia of sensory experiences. This part of the garden has a desert-like quality, enhanced by the agave plants in a bed of pebbles. Leading to the studio, these stepping stones, part of Philip and Graham's ceramic line at Pesamuan, add visual symmetry.

right The wealth of colors and textures imparts yet another aspect to the landscaping on the steep terracing behind the villa.

left Water lilies and tall reeds (*Typha angustifolia*) lend a sublime tranquility to the pond and reflect the traditional *balé* beyond it. The one modern note is in the brightly painted deck chairs.

top Stepping stone blocks counterbalance the fluidity of the water lily pond.

left Philip and Graham have been practicing artists and designers for over 25 years and the gardens of the villa reflect their creative sensibilities. Every detail has been lovingly wrought, from the manicured lawn to the carefully positioned yucca plants and wood "tree" sculptures that evoke the poetry of a Luís Barragan garden.

above The attraction of this corner of the garden lies in the strong symmetry provided by the dividing walls of different heights and in the varied colors and tones used. Terracotta imparts a vivid note, offset by the blue urn and pale gray wall behind it. Pebbles are increasingly the material of choice in modern gardens—easy to maintain, they also offer an attractive display area for shrubs.

a living work of art

The design of The Ritz-Carlton, Bali Resort & Spa draws on a "rice terrace" concept with a myriad of rockeries, fountains and lotus ponds underpinning the importance of water as a main feature in this sumptuous oasis.

right The grounds of the resort feature 19 individual water features and ponds. This vast water lily pond provides a soothing interlude in the gardens.

left The resort garden paths "subliminally" lead guests on a journey from one location to the next and from the private villas to the rest of the resort. About 100,000 square meters of Chandi stone from Borobodur and local Palimanan stone were used throughout the resort. Elegant water features like this one lead the way to the private villas.

below The concept of the resort capitalizes on the magnificent views over the Indian Ocean. The simple lines of the pool complement the traditional Balinese pavilion and stone urns while colorful shrubs merge seamlessly with the expanse of lawn.

living in a light box This house in Singapore designed by Sim Boon Yang of Eco-id Architects employs the principles of *shakkeii*, or "borrowed scenery,"—the Japanese concept of incorporating the surrounding landscape into the garden.

above Blocks of cement, chipped at the edges to resemble stone pillars, artfully divide the car porch from the house.

right The homeowners were passionate about bringing the "outside in and the inside out." When the doors are fully open, the lap pool literally becomes part of the room.

left "The reflections from the pool and the sounds of the water are additional dimensions that help to soften what might seem like a cold, modern house," says the owner. The pool flows over an infinity edge to create a one-storey high waterfall.

making an entrance   The approach to a house is like an introduction to a story—hinting at what lies beyond. Here we showcase the designs of two houses in Singapore by renowned architectural firms, Eco-id Architects and aKTa-rchitects.

above Lending the outside
spaces plenty of personality
are these individual teak wood
posts that mark the boundaries
of the balcony leading from the
living room.
left A rough-hewn granite facade
and teak wood detailing give a
majestic feel to the entrance to
this house designed by Kevin
Tan of aKTa-rchitects. The male
and female stone lions introduce
a traditional element.

right The entrance to this house in Singapore designed by Sim Boon Yang of Eco-id Architects comprises all the elements that constitute a Chinese-inspired garden—water, 11th century stone lions from Cambodia and willowy plants—but with a definitely modern interpretation.
left Three contrasting materials, pebbles, dark wood and stone create a clean yet enticing entrance to the house.
below right In Kevin Tan's design, the pool provides a charming interlude between the living room and granite wall that surrounds the house. An etched stone water feature dominates one end of the pool.
below left Pebbles provide a clever and attractive way to conceal the drain filter, while allowing rainwater to flow away.

secret garden   When the owners of this house in Singapore approached Chan
Soo Khian of SCDA Architects and landscape designer Made Wijaya to work on their
new home, the emphasis was on a natural-looking and easy to maintain garden.

left The entrance to the large house is a beautiful preamble to the interiors. The peacock flower (*Caesalpinia pulcherrima*) makes for a delicate counterpoint to the granite facade.

above There are actually a number of small gardens within the garden in the house. The owners rescued many of their plants from their previous house and re-planted them here.

top Unusual touches such as Made Wijaya's hanging lamp, water feature and wooden bench add a serenity to the pool.
above Slender granite blocks separate the garage from the entrance proper.

right The owners wanted the pool to be in the center of the house, and the starting point for the design. "In the morning, the reflections from the granite walls and wood ceilings are really lovely," says the owner.

downtown modern The beauty of the landscaping and pool areas at Downtown Apartments in Bali designed by Fredo Taffin of Espace Concept lies in the interplay of lush tropical foliage with a thoroughly modern architectural idiom.

right The Downtown villas, located in the heart of chic Seminyak, are a luxurious, contemporary urban resort. The challenge, says the architect was to "maximize a minimum space" and to fit in a 20-meter lap pool and an entertainment area as well as to create "a tropical garden with a sense of depth in a 200-meter-square pad!" Just a step down from the living room, the pool ends with an unusual water feature made of wood and local slate, surrounded by two painted piers.
left Made locally by craftsmen under Fredo Taffin's supervision, the featured wall makes a prominent statement. Each of the walls in the villas plays on different configurations of the raised motifs.
below The stark simplicity of these plants emphasizes the clean lines of the entrance to the villas.

eco-elegance Eco-friendly design is playing an increasingly important role in today's modern gardens. In this house in Singapore, the concept, according to the owners, was to have "an equatorial rainforest to hold all the architecture together."

above Antique wooden columns from India encircle one side of the pool.

right The enormous pool takes center stage in this house which seems to grow out of and from the surrounding greenery. One of the main features of the pool is the fibre-optic lights created by Australian company Lighting Design Partnership. At dusk the lights appear to glow like an exotic species of pond life!

left What the owners love best about this garden is that "it takes us to another world— a world of lushness and controlled wilderness."

urban sanctuary With this house he designed in Singapore, Benny Cheng of space_craft illustrates how an essentially narrow site can be transformed into a chic and stylish city oasis by incorporating the living areas with the garden.

left By extending the decking to the very edge of the pool, the living room becomes an integral part of the landscape and provides the perfect location for al fresco entertaining.

below The granite wall of the outdoor bathroom mirrors the external stepping stones.

opposite Prior to Benny's renovations, the dimensions of the house were small indeed. "It was just a huge backyard before the living room, pool and the master bedroom were constructed," he says. Here, the view from the master bedroom shows the pool and garden where the minimal approach to plant selection accentuates the clean lines of the structure.

The villa Greg Dall of Pentago built in Kuala Lumpur embodies the
"perfect house in the tropics"—one with a minimal number of walls, a roofed space
in landscaped gardens, and water to create a refreshing environment.

right A large earthenware pot set amongst large pebbles provides simple yet striking detailing.
below The pool and patio area connects the living room and the open-plan office. Instead of a traditional Malay-style house, the design that Greg had chosen to adopt was that of modern resort-style living.
left The outdoor terrace is the family's formal dining area. Terracotta walls and antique doors and columns from southern India enhance the vibrant paintings by local artist Ivan Lam. Aquatic arrowheads add an ethereal quality to the pool.

simply natural Increasingly, gardens are becoming our sanctuaries away from the hustle and bustle of everyday life. This tranquil garden in a house in Singapore was a true "labor of love" for interior designer, architect and homeowner HL Lim.

left Having a pool that is an extension of the floor level helps to maintain a homogenous look in the garden. The wooden trellis has a softening effect on the landscaping, mature trees enhance the intimacy of the garden while choosing pots in the same shade of green creates an overall balance and harmony.

above The combination of wood decking on different levels and lush foliage heightens the peaceful aspect of the garden.

skinny dip Designed by David and Pariya Lees, the small cigar shape of this narrow pool in a Bangkok home resulted from the owners' need for a play pool for their children that combined adult elegance and a compact size.

above A Balinese-inspired pond and fountain divide the dining room and pool areas. The fountain consists of Balinese wooden rice pounders set on concrete plinths on top of three ponds filled with a lush profusion of various water lilies, grasses, lotuses, fish and terrapins.

right and left The pool, edged in granite, is screened from the neighboring house with spreading fan palms, haleconia plants and trellising. The pool's seven-meter length does not allow for serious lap swimming, so two water jets were added at one end to provide exercise for swimmers, an idea the owner adopted from small urban pools in Australia.

liquid landscape   Water features are the key landscaping element used to create a modern resort look at the Evason Resort & Spa Hua Hin. This style merges the indoors with the outdoors, echoing the concepts pioneered by Geoffrey Bawa.

left Water is the dominant design element in the spa building. A stone urn reflected in a water tray is a simple but compelling centerpiece in the open-air lobby.
right Massage pavilions in the spa are sunken among water lily ponds, so guests are at eye-level with the pond when lying on the massage table; this adds a fantasy effect of floating on water to the pampering experience.
below left A landscape of reflecting pools replaces the conventional lawn and bushes among the resort buildings. An outdoor corridor leads from the beachfront area to the front of the hotel.
below right Water replaces a conventional floor in the spa, where these dramatic wooden stepping squares lead from the lobby to the massage pavilions.
below far right The massage beds inside the spa's thatched massage pavilions give this frog's eye view of the surrounding lily ponds.

a harmony of space What makes the modern Asian home so engaging is the successful blending of new shapes and volumes within a traditional framework, as the landscaping of this compound in Bali designed by Trevor Hillier demonstrates.

above The megaliths from the island of Flores in Indonesia add a majestic note among the tall coconut palms framing the guest villas.

left Access to the property is across a timber-decked bridge and a pond of water lilies and bull rushes. Trevor wanted "to keep the space open, to allow long views and to maintain the sense of expansiveness."

right Originally, there was little on the land apart from some coconut palms and scrub. They re-planted the whole area with the emphasis on an informal look and functional vegetation that would "screen and subdivide" the compound.

right One of the spectacular features of the pool area is the table made from a single slab of *batu pacitan* which as Trevor explains "was delivered as is from the quarry. It took 47 men to carry it into position." A megalith from Flores adds drama to the space.
left There are two separate villas on the land. This meandering trellis-covered walkway extends from the northern boundary of the property to connect the two houses.
below The essence of oriental grace is captured with this Buddha head at the end of the open corridor across a pond of water canna (*Thalia geniculata*).

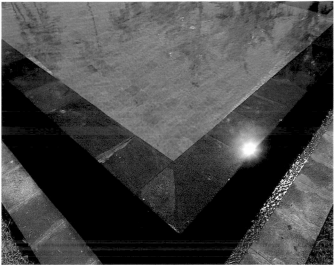

top and above The use of contrasting materials adds interest
to the pool area. The edging is
done in lustrous *batu candi* while
Palimanan Wonosari stone con-
tinues from the decking to the
steps leading down into the pool.
left In keeping with the layout
of the upper house, the pool is
essentially a simple rectangle
with spectacular sea views.
Palimanan Wonosari stone is a
stunning choice for the decking
between the cabana and pool.

in the round Valentina Audrito's design of the three houses that comprise Villa Surga in Bali owe much to her Mediterranean background. In this villa, the concept is "based on soft round shapes that interplay with one another."

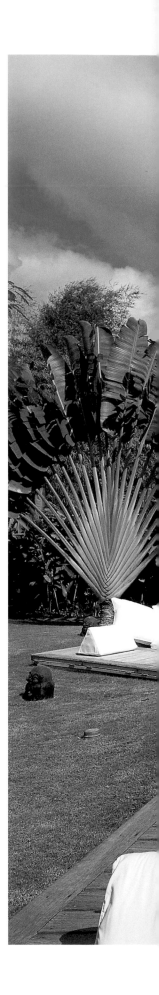

above In designing the villa, Valentina was conscious of the "different levels of the buildings in relation to the garden." She says, "I wanted the volumes to revolve round a focal point—represented by the round living room and the pool and deck—yet face the rice fields."

right White futon cushions and the muslin-clad *balé* create an eye-catching composition against the lush foliage. A pair of traveler's palms add a dramatic note.

left The circular shape and linearity of the pool's design make for a stunning combination.

enchanted garden The magic of Villa Umah di Beji in Bali lies in the tranquility of the setting, the mature garden, numerous water features and the chequered landscaping suggesting a Lewis Carroll-like giant chessboard.

above The owners have imbued the gardens with both traditional and modern stone sculptures, among them this stone gateway overlooking the pool.

right Infinity pools add drama to any contemporary garden.

left One of the focal points of the villa is the rectangular bath or "Beji" swimming pool around which the suites are arranged. Surrounding the well-established garden are numerous points of interest. The *balé* provides for relaxed seating, while modern loungers give uninterrupted views over the pool.

serenity of style   Restaurants and spas are often at the cutting-edge of design as illustrated by The Cliff restaurant designed by Yasuhiro Koichi of Design Studio Spin and the Spa Botanica by Leo Designers at The Sentosa Resort & Spa in Singapore.

left Three ethereal water fountains made from glass adorn the entrance to The Cliff. "I always integrate something symbolic in each of the restaurants I design," says Yasuhiro Koichi, "but the theme is always different. The theme for this restaurant was glass balls."
below right The warm tones of the cascading textured stone wall bring out the opulence of the entrance to the Spa Botanica, created by Leo Designers.
below left These stunning glass balls set in their own pools were designed by Spin and made in Bali by Seiki Torige.

right Playing with vertical lines and planes, this immense rippled stone wall of cascading water makes for an awe-inspiring corridor leading from the interiors of The Cliff to the shallow pools and gardens of the hotel beyond. **below** With the floating granite stepping stones and cascading waterfall on the textured stone wall, Kathy Yuktasevi has introduced an aura of serenity at the entrance of the Spa.

pool perspectives Three essential elements—water, abundant vegetation and spatial harmony—contribute to the stunning visual effect of this garden and pool at Villa Surga in Bali, designed by Valentina Audrito.

left "The round shapes at the end of the pool are there to remind us of the lines of the rice fields that once were there," Valentina says. Stepping stones serve as decking for the pool, which is fashioned from Palimanan stone.
below left The Jacuzzi flows over a waterfall made of a local stone, *batu hijai*, which accentuates the blue tiles used for the interior of the pool.
right "It's all about creating different perspectives from different angles," says Valentina. The starting point and central focus of the design of the garden and pool was the Jacuzzi placed in the middle of the outdoor living space. The back of the Jacuzzi connects with the living room while the front overflows into the pool with views of the romantic *balé* amidst the trees. Valentina's partial Greek heritage contributes to the Hellenic feel of the pool.

chapel of light Ethereal and awe-inspiring, the wedding chapel at Tirtha Uluwatu in Bali, perched high on a cliff overlooking the Indian Ocean, was designed by Glenn Parker of Grounds Kent Architects, and celebrates the best in innovative design.

left Stepping stones over interlocking lakes which lead to and from the chapel seem to disappear into the ocean beyond.
below The nine-meter high chapel, built in Malaysia and assembled in Bali, is made of a steel portal frame draped with Teflon fabric and laminated glass.
opposite "Tirtha" is the Balinese term for holy water. The chapel was designed so that the structure is surrounded on all sides by water. The beautifully wrought stepping stones heighten the "journey" to the chapel.

The shallow pools and low overhanging trees connecting to the wedding chapel cast magical reflections at sunset. A traditional *balé* for outdoor dining faces the diaphanous modern chapel.

family planning Designed by Vitoon Kunalungkarn of IAW in Bangkok, this family pool was designed with the feeling of a resort getaway in mind, as a relief from the highrise urban bustle of the city beyond.

above With the family's young children in mind, the pool was designed with a clearly defined shallow end for the kids and a deep end for adults. The wooden deck offers plenty of room for poolside entertaining.
left A gentle gradation of steps gives plenty of cool seating for chilling by the pool during poolside parties and barbecues.
opposite A wide wooden deck connects the house and pool, defining the pool area outside the family TV room. A stone wall defines a semi-private Jacuzzi area at the deep end of the pool.

a view to thrill Danielle and Mike Mahon's Villa Ylang Ylang in Bali is "a very personal interpretation of western and Asian architecture." The gardens and pool provide a showcase for the couple's impressive sculpture collection.

above The villa is an imposing two-storey open-plan structure with the master and guest bedrooms arranged around the pool. Small frangipani trees add to the overall elegance of design.
left Danielle and Mike have a notable collection of stone statues, mostly from Jogyakarta. Dotted around the lawn, they transform the garden into a sculptural park.
opposite Danielle describes the villa as "a mystical oasis playing with light, smell, sound and touch." The visual focus is on the sea and palm trees. The pool and garden link the different parts of the villa. White Palimanan stone reflects the light.

water tableau Martin Palleros of Tierra Design redesigned the entrance driveway and pool area of The Metropolitan Hotel Bangkok, transforming the old structure into a high-style luxury hotel embodying a calming haven of new international design.

opposite The oxidized brass water tray is a strong landscape element which links the swimming pool, pool deck, restaurant terrace, and entrance court together, while simultaneously dividing them into separate spaces. The water tray floats off the floor to give a clean visual line.

left The water tray punctures the wall, extending into the entrance courtyard. The apertures in the wall suggest an extension of the spaces beyond, so the wall serves as a division without fully enclosing the spaces.

right A low planter at the end of the stone wall divides the entrance courtyard and swimming pool, and facilitates a flow between the two spaces while maintaining privacy for the bathers in the pool area.

left Low plants soften the hard surfaces. Direction signs on the glass fence cleverly transform otherwise banal signage into an element of the landscape design.

far left Overflow from the water tray cascades into the pool, producing a soothing sound effect.

primeval paradise The swimming pool at landscape architect Bill Bensley's residence in Bangkok is an exuberant wonderland of exotic foliage. The expansive pool evokes a tropical lagoon, celebrating the beauty of the region's lushest plants.

above Mimicking nature, the pool's sinuous curves wind into inviting nooks and pockets at every turn.

right Jets of water hidden in the landscaped rocks form a Jacuzzi among the ferns.

left What at first glance looks like a natural jungle is in fact a fantastic example of conscientious landscape design. A whimsical tile frog grins up from the floor of the pool. The roof of the outdoor massage pavilion is visible in the background.

left A towering doorway resembling a fortress portal marks the transition from the entrance courtyard into the garden with much drama. The yellow swirl motif takes its form from the Thai figure for the number "1." **right** A fountain in the shape of a mythological bird adds the soothing sound of falling water to the luscious surroundings.

rocky retreat   An old limestone quarry in Uluwatu in Bali proved the ideal location for architect Giuseppe Verdacchi to design a house that is at once an integral part of the site yet also a very modern structure.

left The house is set on a steep slope, and the positioning of the rooftop swimming pool provides sweeping views of the surrounding countryside. Bougainvillea evokes both the tropics and the sunny Mediterranean coast.

below The limestone quarry the architect found had been extensively mined. The way the stone had been extracted with chisels left beautiful patterns on the rock face, adding to the character of the house.

opposite Viewed from the pool area, the whole site nestles into the rock, creating a tranquil haven. The medley of textures and colors lend a Mediterranean feel to the garden.

a seduction in stone Located near the Tanjung Benoa Beach in Nusa Dua, Bali, the Novotel Benoa designed by architect Lek Bunnag and landscape architect Bill Bensley incorporates the best of traditional Balinese style with a touch of whimsy.

left Understated architecture enhances the beauty of the gardens. The profusion of flowering shrubs and varying levels highlight the large pineapple motifs and female figurines.
below left This bench sculpted in white stone provides an interesting contrast with the surroundings of the pool.
below right Pebbles placed inside the lip of the pool add an unusual touch.
opposite Sculptures abound in the gardens of the hotel. Here a giant female stone statue adorns one end of the pool.

endless blue David Lombardi's home in Bali is testament to the distinctive and inspirational Asian architectural style now emerging, characterized by the interplay of styles and cross-cultural references and the use of diverse materials and shapes.

right The blue walls of this modern and open-plan structure impart a striking contrast with the traditional Alang Alang thatched roofing.
below Ivory-white stepping stones add a pleasing symmetry to the pool. The sudden splashes of color, like the red portal leading to an outside dining space, add a sense of fun to the design.
left The raised rectangular pool overlooks rice fields and a bamboo perimeter fence. The two living areas are connected by a walkway. Seiki Torige's glass panels add a quixotic touch to the Balinese setting.

plane perfection   One of the goals of architectural firm GM is for total harmony between architecture and the environment. In this Bali villa, the restrained lines of the modern structure are reflected in the clean contours of the pool and garden.

above Water plays an integral part in the design of the villa. This organically shaped pool lies between the villa and the garden —the narrow point leads subtly to the living area and gradually widens to include the garden.
right The stunning simplicity of the sculpted pool, the interaction of shapes and volume, as well as the effective use of local stone and wood ensure the enduring modernity of this pool.
left Nestling in the low sloping roofs of the villa that almost sweep the floor, the beautiful coral tree (*Erythrina fusca*) accentuates the intimacy of the overall design.

A well-maintained lawn instantly adds a sense of quietness to any landscape. The frangipani trees and the tactile nature of the rounded stone wall and pristine stepping stones enhance this atmosphere of "softness."

club tropicana   With the design of The Club at The Legian in Bali, architect Shinta Siregar and interior designer Jaya Ibrahim have created private sanctuaries whose "cues for being contemporary are based on eastern aesthetics."

left One of the chief attractions at The Club is the outdoor *balé* with a sunken dining table—perfect for al fresco dining. **below** These day beds carved from wood, ideal for lazing in the sun, adorn the timber terrace. **right** Rather than a sea vista, the views at The Club are centered on the visually elegant but understated drama within the confines of the villas. While adhering to a modern look, a palette of traditional Balinese materials, like coconut wood for the columns and Alang Alang roofs over the *balé*, was specifically chosen. The delicate golden cane palms and leafy shrubs around the pool make for an elegant backdrop.

pools of light Designed by architect Cheong Yew Kuan, Begawan Giri Estate or "Wise Man's Mountain" in Bali is aptly named. This secluded hideaway is set amidst forests, mountains and rice fields and offers the ultimate in peaceful luxury.

above Fashioned from *batu candi*, the pool appears to float above the forest floor. Aged decking evokes the proximity of nature.
right The sharp clean lines of the pool edges are softened by the wooden decking.
left This residence on the estate is called "Tirta Ening" or "Clear Water," and water is indeed the main element throughout. The pavilion at the end of this infinity pool imparts a Zen-like tranquility. African tulip, albizia palms and rain trees add grandeur.

views on the pool   "Modern tropical architecture that includes the pool and external landscaping as part of the spatial quality of the house," is how architect Richard Ho describes this Singapore house he designed for Lars and Serene Sorensen.

right The outdoor "living" room has all the elegance of an indoor space with dark chocolate blinds and modern outdoor furniture from Natural Living.

below These "floating" steps are a major feature of the swimming pool.

left With the majority of the rooms looking onto it, "the swimming pool is the centerpiece and focus of the house," says Richard. The sandblasted granite floor leading to the outdoor living space echoes the granite used on the exterior of the house.

living openly The dramatically modern architectural style of this house in Singapore, designed by Sim Boon Yang of Eco-id Architects, is balanced by the tranquility of this secluded garden and pool.

top Baskets of orchids and a "modern rustic" dining table highlight the contemporary Asian table settings.

above This secluded lounging platform under the shelter of an exquisite sea grape tree the owners found in Muar, Malaysia exudes serenity. The tree also provides a real link between the living room and the garden.

left The owners "wanted to have a serious engagement with the outdoors." The wall of the living room therefore opens up completely so the pool becomes part of the room. Bamboo set in black pebbles is the ideal choice to reflect the oasis-like feel of the garden.

bukit drama   The rugged landscape on Jimbaran Peninsula in Bali proved the perfect location for The Bale. Landscape architect Karl Princic and architect Antony Liu "wanted the resort to appear as if it was carved out of a hillside of stone."

right Water played an important role in the design. "I used water to visually and physically link the lower part of the site with the upper," explains Karl Princic.
left The main pool is located near the top of the site and at the heart of the resort. As Karl explains, "we conceived it as the 'source' for all other water features throughout the site." The different levels and planter boxes provide for private spaces while the various plants, including white bougainvillea, Balinese plumeria, *jati mas* and fountain grass, enhance the intimacy of the pool.
below Karl chose black river pebbles for the floor of the reflecting ponds "to soften them and to create texture."

above Different levels and layers add drama to the overall design. Paras Jogja stone emphasizes the clean strong architectural lines. The raised pool cascades down into another pool below (seen opposite).

left Stepping down into the swimming pool directly from the villa blurs the boundaries between inside and out.

opposite This unique villa gives the impression of stepping into a private world. As Karl explains, the villa "has a lot of interest because of the dramatic changes in level which are directly applied in the swimming pool design." White frangipani and bougainvillea echo the stone utilized throughout the villa.

left The design of The Bale and the selected plants reflect the *bukit* landscape which is typically arid. Water, whether in pools or as water features like this one, plays an integral part in the design precisely because of its natural scarcity in the peninsula.

right The high hillside location of The Bale with ocean views lends itself to the magnificent central "corridor" where the water cascades down the site toward the lobby. "We wanted the resort to appear as if it was carved out of a hillside of stone," says Karl Princic.

below "The architecture is so strong that we wanted the landscape to stand in contrast," says Karl, thus the inclusion of plants and shrubs which required minimal maintenance and "may even look a little unkempt."

contemporary calm   A sense of tranquility and subdued calm are the moods
evoked by the landscape design of Avalon and The Loft Condominiums, two projects
in Singapore designed by Martin Palleros of Tierra Design.

left and far right The communal
pool at Avalon is the central
feature of the landscape. This
granite wall is reminiscent of a
checkerboard, a motif repeated
in the stepping stones. The blend
of plants, granite textures and
water in a balance of vertical and
horizontal lines creates an aura
of poised serenity in the city.
above and right The landscape at
The Loft Condominium in Nassim
Hill is integrated into the architecture. The linearity of the pool and
long wooden deck enhances the
dialog between the old Tembusu
trees at one end of the pool, and
the newly introduced trees at the
other end. The long stone wall
punctuated with green plants is a
contrast to the site's natural feel.

At The Loft Condominium, willowy 100-year-old Tembusu trees give the site its essence of gentle tranquility. The landscape design concept was to incorporate as many of the old trees as possible so as to emphasize the site's existing character.

river dance The riverbank location of this residence in Kanchanaburi, Thailand, designed by Martin Palleros of Tierra Design, is a key element in establishing the visual and spatial relationship between the buildings and grounds.

above This property consists of guest villas on a site next to the client's private residence, and is conceptualized as a fully integrated series of living and garden spaces. The buildings connect visually and physically to the landscape, with timber screens that open up to the river view, and with stone urns and wooden plinths establishing the link.
opposite An elevated expanse of manicured lawn provides a strong central area while drawing the eye toward the tranquil river. This space was also created

as an area to display outdoor sculptures. To strengthen the link with the river, the water feature was designed with an infinity edge to fuse visually with the site's key feature—the river's edge. Playful stepping stones lead to a meditation pavilion.
right A formal entrance zone and driveway is framed by free-standing walls with apertures offering hints of the landscape beyond. The space's stark geometry is softened by a fountain and the gentle sound of water cascading from stone water spouts into a long, raised reflecting tray.

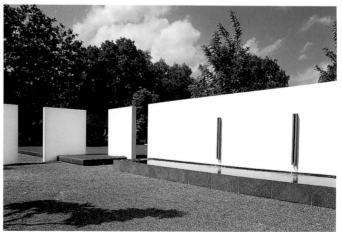

The swimming pool was designed to merge seamlessly with the landscape, so that it looks more like a pond than a swimming pool. Towering tamarind trees provide a foliate canopy while the smaller flowering frangipani trees within the grounds form the link between the landscape and buildings on a more human scale. The lawn was raised to define the line between the man-made and natural landscapes.

sculptural settings Richard North-Lewis of Sabita Design conceptualized this limestone wall at the entrance to the seriously stylish bar and restaurant in Bali. He says, "It was anti-tradition, which I thought fitted in with the ideals of Ku de Ta."

top and above Richard's design was inspired by New York subway graffiti, the modern library in Alexandria and "a desire to create something very different from the usual Balinese designs." He adds, "There are over 200 individual pieces which I hope represent a board spectrum of emotions from kissing seahorses to a 17th century Creed Indian message about the environment."
left A concrete fountain set in pebbles from Flores makes a stunning impact at the entrance.

The authors would like to express their thanks to the following people who gave their kind support during the production of this book:

BALI
Valentina Audrito, Arthur Chondros at Downtown Apartments, Jaya Ibrahim, Anjarini Kencahyati, Philip Lakeman and Graham Oldroyd, Mike and Danielle Mahon, Hans-Jörg Meier at The Legian, Richard North-Lewis of Sabita Design, Glenn Parker, Karl Princic of Karl Princic Design, Fredo Taffin at Espace Concept, the staff at Tirtha Uluwatu, David Wilson at The Ritz-Carlton, Bali Resort & Spa and Gill Wilson.

Antony Liu Budiwihardja Jl Raya Perjuangan, Kompleks Plaza Kebun, Jeruk Blok E-11, Jakarta Barat 11530, tel: (62) 021 535 0319/25/34, email: tonton@dnet.net.id

Bensley Design Studios Jl Batur Sari, Gang SK IX No 3, Sanur Bali, tel: (62) 361 281 413, email: bdsbali@denpasar.wasantara.net.id; bdsdps@telkom.net

Cheong Yew Kwan email: area@indo.net.id

David Lombardi email: dave@fullondesign.com

Fredo Taffin Espace Concept, 250 Beddington Rd, Noosa Heads Doonan 4562, Queensland Australia, www.espaceconcept.net

Giuseppe Verdacchi email: verdachi@indosat.net.id

GKA Jl Raya Legian No 362, Legian, Kecamatan Kuta Denpasar 80361 Bali, tel: (62) 361 763 064/65, email: gkabali@indosat.net.id

Glenn Parker email: gpai@indosat.net.id

GM email: gmarc@tiscalinet.it

Jaya Pratomo Ibrahim email: jayaibrahim@jaya-associates.com

Karl Princic Design PT Intaran Asri, Landscape Architecture and Resort Planning, 47A Jl Batursari, Sanur Bali, tel: (62) 361 286 462, fax: (62) 361 286 463, email: kpd@idola.net.id; kpd@dps.centrin.net.id

Nexus Studio Architects Perkantoran Duta Wijaya, Unit 1, Jl Raya Puputan, Denpasar Bali, tel: (62) 361 744 3493, email: nexus@dps.centrin.net.id

Pesamuan Jl Pungutan 25, Sanur Bali, www.pesamuan-bali.com

PT Alindi Kyati Praya email: alindi@indosat.net.id

PT. Wijaya Tribwana International email: ptwijaya@indosat.net.id

Sabita Design PO Box 148, Nusa Dua 80363, Bali, tel/fax: (62) 361 701 597, email: sabitadesign@telkom.net; northlewisdesign@hotmail.com

Seiki Torige Galeri Esok Lusa, Jl Raya Basangkasa 47, Seminyak Kuta, 80361 Bali, tel/fax: (62) 361 735 262, email: gundul@eksadata.com

Valentina Audrito tel: (62) 812 390 9614/(62) 361 743 2557, email: vale-studio65@dps.centrin.net.id; vaudrito@hotmail.com

MALAYSIA
Greyy Dall of Pentago.

Pentago 21-11 The Boulevard, Midvalley City, Lingkaran Syed Putra, 59200 Kuala Lumpur, tel: (65) 05 2282 3188, fax (65) 05 2282 2016, email: info@pentago.com.my

SINGAPORE
Kevin Tan of aKTa-rchitects, Jean Khoo of City Developments, Sim Boon Yang and Calvin Sim of Eco-id Architects, Richard Ho of RichardHo Architects, Trevor Hillier of One Degree North, Anthony Ross and Yong Han Weelin of Sentosa Resort and Spa, Benny Cheng of space_craft and Stan and Geri Lee of Watermount Gardens.

aKTa-rchitects 25 Seah St #05-01, S'pore 188381, tel: (65) 6333 4331, www.akta.com.sg

Design Studio Spin email: spin@msb.biglobe.ne.jp

Eco-id Architects 11 Stamford Rd, #04-06, Capitol Bldg, S'pore 178884, tel: (65) 6337 5119, email: ecoid@pacific.net.sg

Leo Designers #09-03 219 Henderson Rd, S'pore 159556, tel: (65) 6272 7371, fax: (65) 6276 3977, email: leo@lidgintl.com

One Degree North Landscape Architects email: onedegreenorth@pacific.net.sg

RichardHo Architects 691 East Coast Rd, S'pore 459057, tel: (65) 6446 4811, email: rharch@pacific.net.sg

SCDA 10 Teck Lim Rd, S'pore 088386, tel: (65) 6324 5458, www.scdaarchitects.com

Sottsass Associati www.sottsass.it

space_craft 324 River Valley Rd, S'pore 238356, tel: (65) 6333 3108, www.spacecraft.com.sg

Watermount Gardens 1 Pandan Valley #01-104, S'pore 597625, tel: (65) 9178 1810, email: wtmount@singnet.com.sg

Natural Living 9 Penang Rd, #03-01 Park Mall, S'pore 238459, tel: (65) 6334 8928, email: info@natural-living.com.sg, www.natural-living.com.sg

THAILAND
Diana Moxon of Anantara Resort & Spa Hua Hin, Bill Bensley of Bensley Design Studios, Eva Malmstrom Shivdasani of Six Senses Hotels & Resorts, Arthur Napolitano, Rika Dila, Martin Palleros of Tierra Design, Debbie Thio and Supranee Taecharungroj of The Metropolitan Bangkok, Nachanok Ratchanadaros of Extase Restaurant.

Bensley Design Studios 57 Soi Sukhumvit 61, Sukhumvit Rd, Bangkok 10110, Thailand, tel: (662) 381 6305, fax: (662) 381 6647, email: bensley@mozart.inet.co.th, www.bensley.com

IAW Soi Panich-Anan Sukhumvit 71, Bangkok 10110, tel: (662) 713 1237, fax: (662) 713 1238, email: iawbkk@loxinfo.co.th

Tierra Design 1 Leura St, Nedlands, Western Australia 6009, tel: (618) 9389 7933, fax: (618) 9389 7922, email: perth@tierradesign.com, www.tierradesign.com

PHILIPPINES
Eckard Rempe of The Farm at San Benito.